Frances Margaret Tener Milne

Heliotrope

A San Francisco Idyl

Frances Margaret Tener Milne

Heliotrope
A San Francisco Idyl

ISBN/EAN: 9783744661638

Printed in Europe, USA, Canada, Australia, Japan

Cover: Foto ©ninafisch / pixelio.de

More available books at **www.hansebooks.com**

Heliotrope

A SAN FRANCISCO IDYL

TWENTY-FIVE YEARS AGO

AND OTHER SKETCHES

BY

Mrs. FRANCES MARGARET MILNE

Author of "For To-Day," and "A Cottage Gray."

SAN FRANCISCO
THE STAR PUBLISHING COMPANY
1897

COPYRIGHT, 1897
BY FRANCES MARGARET MILNE

TO EDITH

WHOSE BEAUTIFUL AND HAPPY GIRLHOOD HAS EVER PROVED
HER TENDER SYMPATHY FOR OTHERS, THESE
SKETCHES ARE LOVINGLY INSCRIBED

AUNT FRANCES

CONTENTS.

Heliotrope	9
A May Basket	27
"Home, Sweet Home"	47
Her Neighbor	57
Broken Promises	95

HELIOTROPE.

" There my Heliotrope, like a saint, death-faint,
  Feared that radiant azure to paint
  Where glimmer the mansions of rest;
Yet, for all her pale doubting, did bear, unaware,
  A heaven in her breast,
And we leaned and we longed in that heaven to share."

IT was such a sad change to Bess from the pretty cottage garden in lovely Santa Rosa, with its clustering roses and glowing masses of flowers, to the four small rooms of this city "flat," with its "upstairs yard" behind, where not a foot of soil was found to offer welcome to any of Mother Earth's sweet children.

To be sure, there was the exciting variety of city streets and gay shop-windows, and the novel experience of the great school, any one of whose rooms seemed almost as large as the whole school-house in her own town, and among whose innumerable throng of pupils she felt at first quite lost and bewildered. But none of these made up to Bess for the fresh, pure air and open fields. She was a wise and thoughtful little soul; and it was not long before she began to realize that, unless on the rare occasion when she went with mamma "down town," there was not much glory or bliss in a city life, when it meant living ever so far out on one of the street car lines (there were none but the slow, old-fashioned horse-cars, then), and climbing that long, dreary flight of stairs to the rooms called home. The wide, shady streets and the vine-embowered dwellings, and the large, old-fashioned plaza with its careless stretch of grass and clumps of live oaks, would have far more than reconciled her to the loss of an occasional glimpse through those gorgeous thoroughfares of Market and Kearny streets, where, on a Saturday afternoon, she had sometimes watched the richly-dressed ladies who thronged out of the theatres at the matinee's close.

The one real delight Bess had known during those first six months in San Francisco had been the May-day festival at Woodward's Gardens (the dear old gardens are gone, now!) How she had enjoyed that day! And truly it was a beautiful sight to see the crowds of school-children, with their mothers and teachers (who were all admitted free), pouring into the spacious and handsome grounds, parting and meeting in mutual delight as they roamed from one object of interest to another; now watching the sea-lions' uncouth gambols, disporting in the great basin; now walking through the cool, rocky corridor of the aquarium, and pausing in rapt delight before the silvery trout flashing back and forth in their crystal prison, or turning with shuddering disgust from the cruel shark who seemed to follow the gazer enviously with its evil eye. But the loveliest picture of all—a rapture both for eye and ear—was the extensive aviary, enclosed with its light and beautiful wire railing, within whose generous confines the birds soared and sang unconscious of captivity. Bess hardly knew whether to linger longest here or in the conservatory, where every flower and shrub seemed calling her to stay. She looked with longing eyes at the foliage and bloom, as the gardener carefully watered and arranged the stands of potted plants.

"Oh, mamma," she said as they sat down to lunch in one of the arbors, "if I only had one little plant, even in the tiniest flower-pot! It would have a little earth about it—it is so dismal never to see a bit of earth; only boards, boards!"

Mamma laughed at her little girl's tragic tone. "It will be still more dismal to have a discontented daughter," she said, patting her darling's cheek. "But I know my Bess does not mean to be that; only since she cannot have her own little garden now, from which to gather any of her favorite blossoms, she must try all the more to be a fragrant little house-flower herself, and make home sweet and glad and bright for papa and mamma."

But I am sure mamma must have pondered over that pitiful lament: "It is so dismal never to see a bit of earth," as mammas do ponder over the sayings and wishes of their little ones, for one morning nearly a month later, when Bess awoke, she almost thought she must be dreaming still, or back again in dear Santa Rosa, for there was the loveliest perfume floating through the room; and, as she rubbed her sleepy eyes, she saw on the stand beside her bed the cunningest little flower-pot with a plant of heliotrope in full bloom, seeming to waft her "good-morning" from every scented petal.

I can tell you Bess was up and dressed very quickly that morning; and what a happy little girl it was that came into the kitchen where mamma was laying the table for breakfast!

"Oh, what a beauty, mamma!" she cried, setting her treasure very carefully on the broad sill of the open window. And then two plump arms were thrown around mamma's neck, and two sweet kisses gave her loving thanks.

But it would not do to deny one of California's floral children the air and sun of heaven; a poor prisoned house-plant would have had few charms for Bess. "It would seem like a caged bird," she said. And so papa made a little shelf just outside the kitchen door, low enough for Bess to reach but yet a trifle higher than the close wooden railing which enclosed that small upstairs yard which Bess had described so opprobriously as "all boards."

No one but mamma could have understood fully the intense pleasure it was to Bess to gently stir the earth around the tender roots of her beloved plant; to watch its healthy growth, and rejoice in the deepening green of the leaf and delicate lavender tint of the blossom.

Papa must have one in his button-hole every morning, and mamma's dress was not complete without a tiny spray fastened in the modest lace fichu. Anything to equal the pride and satisfaction of Bess in beholding these adornments it were difficult to imagine.

"Poor child," mamma said to herself, between a smile and a sigh, "it does seem cruel not to gratify such an innocent natural longing."

And she and papa had begun to hold secret counsel whether it were not possible to compass a miniature garden by transforming a certain long empty box into that "thing of beauty"; papa thought he could get the earth to fill it from one of the new parks; when suddenly, one morning, this little idyl of happiness centered in a solitary flower-pot was changed to woeful tragedy.

PART II.

Out of her first sound sleep that July night, Bess had wakened with a smothering sense of the changed, dry atmosphere that betokened the coming of a dreaded north wind—the sirocco of California.

"Oh, my poor heliotrope," was her first thought, as she heard the gale rising; "it will be all withered. If I had only brought it in!"

She got up softly and looked out into the hall. It was quite dark only for a faint glimmer from mamma's night lamp that showed through a half-open door. But Bess knew the way so well she felt sure she could reach the kitchen without making any noise, and rescue her treasure from its peril. Her little bare feet stole along the passage, and with eager anxiety she found her hand at last upon the handle of the outer door. Lightly slipping the bolt, she threw it open and reached out on tiptoe to grasp her precious flower-pot—but the shelf was empty.

"The wind has knocked it off," she

thought, with the first thrill of disappointment. "Oh, it will be all broken!"

She stepped quite outside the door now, her little white figure showing plainly in the dim light. There was no moon, but the stars were shining brilliantly in a sky of crystalline blue from which that searching wind had swept every trace of cloud. Bess could see the floor of the yard plainly enough, but just close to the house it lay in shadow; and down she went on her knees, feeling around with groping little hands that trembled with chill and grief; but not an atom of her vanished heliotrope could she find. A narrow street ran along that side of the house—a blind alley—giving access to the back of both upper and lower floors of the houses on either side. "Could the wind have blown it clear over?" was her next horrified thought. "No, it couldn't; yes, it could too; for the shelf is just a little higher than the railing. If I had only asked papa to put it lower!"

But peer as she might into the depths below, it was not possible to fathom its secrets; and just then she heard papa's voice saying:

"Where in the world does this wind come

from? I declare the kitchen door must be open!"

And she flew back to close it, stopping at mamma's door to call out:

"It is only me, papa; oh, mamma, my heliotrope is gone!"

Her voice was all broken and sobbing with cold and distress.

"Bessie," said mamma, sitting up to catch a sight of her, "is it possible you have been standing out there in your night dress? You will get your death of cold, child. Now, run right back to bed and cover up warm."

"Yes, mamma," Bess answered with shivering obedience; and then, still fain to be comforted, "Do you think it is lost, mamma?"

"No, no, dear; I guess not. We'll find it in the morning. Run along now, and go to sleep."

And Bess cuddled down forlornly in her little nest, and sobbed herself into the land of dreams.

Such curious dreams! She thought she was walking along the streets of a beautiful city, but it was not a bit like this "dusty and gusty" city of San Francisco; and it was not either like her dear Santa Rosa. There were beautiful wide lawns on either hand where little children played and sang and gathered flowers that shone all over the rich, soft grass, like jewels set in emerald; and there were the stateliest buildings, through whose doors people were constantly coming and going, and everybody seemed busy without hurry; and when you heard their voices speaking to each other it was like music, for indeed it was the music of love. And there was the loveliest ripple of water from sparkling streams that ran like clear crystal over their shining beds; and the trees were full of blossoms and fruit.

A strange sort of trembling seized the heart of our poor little Bess to find herself in such a heavenly place, when, all at once, her eyes caught sight of what seemed at first to be her very own heliotrope. Yes, that was surely the same little flower-pot with that three-cornered nick in the side she could remember so well; and there were the very number of stems she counted yesterday. But how did it come to be placed in the window of that beautiful mansion?

And then one of the happy people of the place (they made Bess think of Bunyan's "shining ones," there was such a glory of love and peace all about them) came to the window, leading a pale girl, and seated her on a soft couch of repose. "For her toil is over now," Bess heard sweet voices say, "and it is our Brother's will that she should rest and be comforted."

And Bess noticed that the girl's face had a strange new look of dawning joy, and that her eyes had the luster of "clear shining after rain"; and she raised her thin hand, and touched the heliotrope with loving fingers, and at that touch the simple little flower burst forth into such bloom as it had never known on earth, and the little clay flower-pot changed and glowed until it shone like clear gold.

Bess cried aloud in her wonder and delight, and with the cry she woke; but, half-dreaming still, she cried and cried again, "Oh, let me stay there too!"

And then, out of the distance, faint and far, those heavenly voices seemed to answer, "Not yet, little sister; not yet. But thou shalt come when our Lord calls, for of such is His Kingdom."

And then like the fuller swell of some rejoicing anthem, came the words, "Forasmuch as ye did it to the least of these, ye did it unto Me."

And Bess sat up in her little bed, dazed and awe-struck, while the bright morning sunshine streamed through the curtains and fell upon her Testament lying open on the table where mamma had left it the evening before, after reading their good-night verse. Bess looked instinctively at the page, and read there again the verse of her dream.

It was more than a week after, and Bess was almost beginning to forget, in the throng of her busy little life, that beautiful vision of her slumber when, one afternoon returning from school, she happened, for some reason, to go into the house by the back way; and as she passed along that narrow, blind alley, she chanced to look across to the other side, and there, on the window sill, stood a flower-pot with a plant in full bloom, the sight of which made her little heart stand still.

Yes, it could be no other; the very air carried the tidings to her in that sweet, caressing perfume; it was—it surely was—her own lost heliotrope! There was the three-cornered nick in the edge of the pot, that she remembered so well; there was the letter "B" she had tried to carve upon it, as sign of ownership; and, as to her darling flower itself, Bess felt she could have sworn to every leaf and blossom.

The window was open, for it was a sultry day, and within the room a girl of perhaps eighteen had wheeled her sewing-machine close up to it, and sat with bowed head, so absorbed in her task that she did not notice Bess standing in rooted astonishment across the way. But after the first surprised moment, as Bess started forward with a sudden natural impulse of claiming her own, she raised her eyes, with the sense of another presence, and stayed her foot for an instant on the treadle; and in that instant Bess saw, with a leaping heart-thrill, the worn, mortal face of the pale, transfigured girl who had glorified her dream.

"Would you like a flower?" the sewing-girl asked, mistaking Bess's silence as she paused beside the window for bashful admiration.

She put out her hand to break off a spray,

and the thin face lit up with a smile of wondrous sweetness. Once again her dream took living form to Bess; she almost looked to see the plant bloom with celestial blossom as those frail fingers touched it, and that earthen vase to glow with golden light.

"Isn't it lovely?" the girl went on; "I put it on the stand beside poor father's bed sometimes," pointing to a curtained corner of the room. "Poor father! he is blind and cannot see it, but he loves to touch the leaves and smell the flowers, and it helps him to forget the pain."

"Indeed, it is beautiful," stammered Bess; she had no longer any thought that it was hers.

"Oh, mamma," she said that evening, sobbing out her little tale in those loving arms, "it seemed as if it had been given to her without me; only I could have cried for joy that it was hers."

"But the most curious thing of all," the girl added, "is how I came to have it. It doesn't really belong to me at all. The morning after that high wind, a week ago, I found it in a corner of our yard, not much the worse for its journey, only a stem or two broken; and I put it in a sheltered place against the wall, and I watered and straightened it until now it is as good as new. And to-day I thought how I had no real right to keep it, and so I set it here, thinking the owner might happen to pass. But it will seem very lonesome to father and me when it is gone."

"Oh, she could never take it now," Bess said hastily. "I—I—I mean—whoever it belongs to—they could not have the heart. And see how it grows with you—just as if it loved you!"

"I am sure that I love it, anyway," was the answer. She handed Bess the little spray of green and lavender; and then her tireless foot pressed the treadle again, eager to regain lost time, and Bess felt she could interrupt her no longer.

But her young thoughtful eyes had noticed many things during that brief talk. It was leather, not cloth, that was passing with steady persistence under the firm foot of that machine; but how different the heavy, monotonous sound of the treadle was to the noiseless swiftness of mamma's "Domestic." What a poor, poor room it was, too—how bare of any real comfort—

of which she had caught a glimpse! Bess had been wont to think their own home sometimes bare enough; but this was poverty itself. And why did that girl draw her breath with that gasping sigh? Why did she sometimes press her hand against her side? Mamma would know; she would help her to get well.

Indeed, it was not long before mamma was a trusted friend across the way; and what tender, willing hearts could compass out of narrow means to soothe those darkening days was done. For Bess saw that mamma's face grew sadder daily, as she watched the window across the way, or returned from the visit there, snatched from her own busy cares; and then, at last, the ceaseless hum of that sewing-machine was silenced, never to sound again; and the door opened for the weary form of the old man to pass to death's merciful rest. While within, on her scanty bed, the faithful daughter lay down at last, her work completed, content that God had strengthened her to its end.

And days of suffering and days of peace succeeded, until that morning when Bess stood, with quivering lips, beside her mother, with a sacred grief and joy too deep for tears or wailing, and looked upon the quiet face and closed eyes, beside whose deep repose the heliotrope still bloomed.

"She has gone home," mamma said softly, smoothing the fair hair; and again Bess seemed to hear the words:

"For her toil is over; and it is our Brother's will that she should rest and be comforted."

A MAY BASKET.

*"Who ever strove
To show her merit, that did miss her love?"*

*"The flowers in silence seemed to breathe
Such thoughts as language could not tell."*

THERE was a great stillness in the school-room that morning, and a look of half-nervous expectation on every face—a look of sympathy and kindness, certainly, but yet not of delight.

Miss Langton, the teacher, had been seriously ill for over two months, and this was the first day since her recovery that she was to take charge of her pupils again. All the girls, big and little, were tenderly glad-hearted to know that she was well; but they felt, with a secret pang, how happy those two months had been, with what untired feet they had climbed the hill of knowledge under a guidance they loved. Their teacher's place, during that interval of illness, had been supplied by Miss Morton, who had charge of the class-room where the younger scholars of the upper rooms recited; they had all been familiar, in their turn, with her firm and gentle rule; even the triumph of advance and success had not hindered the sense of regret with which they quitted her for Miss Langton's higher grade. Isabel Morton was certainly one of those rare and gifted teachers who, like poets, are born, not made; she had the subtle faculty of imparting knowledge as if she herself were gaining it along with you; and it was a common tribute to her worth for one of the girls to say, "I never could understand that Rule of Three till Miss Morton taught me," or "I always blundered in my parsing till I joined Miss Morton's grammar class."

The sense of comradeship blended thus with respect for authority and superior learning; and a genuine affection—in some instances, almost a passionate regard of reverence and love—bound these young hearts to her own. Her wise and loving rule knew no favoritism, and caused no jealousy; and if, as was doubtless the case, there were one or two among her pupils peculiarly endeared to her by some especial sweetness of disposition and readiness of thought, the duller, or less amiable, never realized the difference by any invidious distinction of preferment, but were drawn on, insensibly, to wish and strive for truer excellence themselves.

There were legends afloat, too, in this little world, of tender, humble ministries among the poor and needy, of kindness bestowed out of her narrow means, that surrounded the fair, bright face of the young teacher with something of the halo of a saint; it had been whispered among the girls that Miss Langton's salary had gone on without abatement during this tedious illness, through the generous contrivance of her associate, who had managed, at the same time, to secure for one of the elder girls a long-coveted opportunity to test her ability in teaching—by resigning to her care her own class-room, while she took charge of the larger and more responsible department of the absent lady principal, with no addition to her own small monthly payment—glad to think that the larger sum would help to lighten the burden and expense of that heavy illness, and that the weary hours of convalescence would not be shadowed by any fear of losing position and income. And, indeed, those two months, overflowing with work and anxiety as they had been, had yet proved very happy ones to her, as well as to her "girls"; that large, cheerful school-room had never witnessed sunnier hours than these, while February snows and March winds had tried in vain for entrance. But now the old order must return; and Miss Morton's genuine happiness, and look of sweet content, as she entered that April morning, with their long-absent teacher leaning on her arm, roused the girls to almost a sudden sense of shame for their indulged regret. And, indeed, the pale, thin face which looked at them with wistful eyes, over the official desk, appealed to their young sympathy with unresisted pathos; many an old score of fancied petulance and injustice was wiped out at the sight, and softened feeling resolved that no thoughtless annoyance should try the strength of that wasted frame.

For, truth to tell, Maria Langton was emphatically a teacher made, not born. Thrust by untoward fate into a calling for which, even in her youth, she felt no glow of enthusiasm, she had struggled bravely on, through infirmities of temper and of will, yet with a conscientious endeavor to fulfill her trust, until middle life still found her straining at the oar of a vocation which had indeed become a duty, and a habit strong as second nature, but which had never been her pleasure or her choice.

As she glanced over the room this morning, in answer to the murmured greeting of her pupils, her eyes looked dull and sad; she pined for love, she felt the chill of its absence, yet knew not how to gain the coveted blessing. A cruel sense of contrast was tormenting her soul; she had watched, with almost jealous pain, many a time and oft, how those clear eyes would kindle and those soft cheeks flush as Isabel Morton called her class; she was imagining, now, the fervor of rejoicing with which that beloved presence would have been welcomed back. How different from the decorous, timid, half-whispered congratulations which had met herself.

The foolish, unreasonable pain at her heart found utterance in words as foolish; and yet I know not, judged by results, whether to call them foolish or wise.

"I know very well, girls," she said at the close of the morning session, "that you are all sorry to lose Miss Morton and have me back instead, but we have no choice in the matter ourselves, so you must make the best of it as well as I."

There was a startled pause in the gathering together of books preparatory to dismissal; some eyes looked down abashed, with a confused sense of blame; some were raised in frank surprise; while not a few exchanged glances of astonishment and question; but no reply was possible, and in a few moments the usual orderly procession filed out of the room.

Only one girl, May Manning, lingered behind. She had a little message to deliver, and, as Miss Langton rose to put on her cloak, she came up to the platform and said with modest sweetness:

"Mamma told me to give you her love, Miss Langton, and to say how happy she is to know of your recovery. I am very glad, too; it seems so natural to have our own teacher back."

Maria's lips trembled. She was not so strong as before her illness, and the morning had been one of suppressed agitation to her. She murmured some fitting answer to Mrs. Manning's kind remembrance, "and you too, my dear, thanks for your kind welcome." She held out her hand, bending towards the girl, who stood a step below her. May colored as she took it in her own warm clasp, and, yielding to a sudden impulse, raised her head and softly kissed her teacher's cheek, then with shy swiftness hurried away.

Poor Miss Langton! Her lip trembled still more piteously, and a few hot tears followed her smothered sob.

PART II.

There was no lack of comment and discussion outside.

"What a strange thing for Miss Langton to say!" cried Ada Leigh. "But she always was nervous and fidgety. I thought a pity of her, too; she looks so ill yet."

"I didn't," replied a bolder spirit—Emma Coxe. "I think it was very unjust as well as ridiculous. How are we to blame, if we do love Miss Morton best? People must be lovable, if they are to be loved. As long as we obey her rules and learn our lessons, I don't see what business it is of hers how we feel towards her."

"I think it was very absurd, too; and yet it made me feel very uncomfortable, as if I had been unkind and hard-hearted," added Rebecca Stone.

"It was so very undignified," said Gertrude Daun. "A teacher who can forget herself so is unfit for her place. If Miss Langton would just take notice how calm and impartial Miss Morton is, as well as so affectionate and kind, she could discover the secret of our preference. But she is so capricious and fretful—never two days alike. I wish I was out of it altogether, and into the High School."

"Oh, Gertie dear, that is surely an exaggeration," exclaimed May Manning, whose delayed footsteps had just caught up with the group. "You know Miss Langton never does stint praise when she thinks it is deserved; and she is so proud of us when we do well. Don't you remember that last visit of the Directors? how she made you read over that beautiful composition you wrote, and had Ada bring out her map, and Emma her copy book? She had something kind to say to all of us, I think, after they had gone, and then thanked us so warmly for the good order we kept while they were there."

"But you know she *is* capricious, and very cross, too, sometimes," Gertie interposed, but with a somewhat mollified tone of voice; indeed, the soft answer that turneth away wrath was beginning to have its effect all round.

"Oh, well, may be we'll be cross too after a while, those of us who get to be teachers," laughed May. "If I had to teach any one so stupid as I am sometimes, I know I should be."

"Well, May Manning, when you get cross, we may all be excused," the girls cried in chorus, for May's sweetness of temper was proverbial.

"We can't wait now," May continued, as they reached the street corner where their paths parted; "but I have been thinking of something all morning—only it's a secret. Wait for me after school, girls; I want to tell you about it."

You may be sure the prospect of sharing a secret called together an eager conclave as soon as school was over, and their steps were as slow as their tones were animated, as they paced homeward discussing May's proposal.

"To tell the truth, girls," she began, "I think we are a little to blame about Miss Langton. It isn't that we ought to love Miss Morton less, but we might try to love Miss Langton a little more. Just think, if we were only loved, all of us, in proportion to our goodness, where would we be? And I suppose she is a little cross some times, and can't make you feel so *one* with her as Miss Morton does, yet what a good faithful teacher she has been all these years—so conscientious and anxious for our improvement. I went to school before papa moved here, where the teacher never seemed to care whether we knew our lessons or not; but then she was very good-natured. For my part, I would rather be scolded sometimes than neglected and have my time wasted like that."

"Yes, that is true," Emma assented, with murmuring concurrence from the others.

"I have often heard mamma say," observed Ada, "what a good daughter and sister Miss Langton is; and how, since she was only fifteen, she has been the main dependence of her widowed mother, and helped to provide for all the family."

"And she showed wonderful self-denial, too," said Rebecca. "Just look how fond she is of books and music and lectures, and yet she hardly ever enjoys them; even her drawing, that she is so clever at, she has not pursued, as she must have longed to do, because she wanted to pay for her little sister's lessons with that Mr. B—, and he said little Ruth had real genius."

"You see," May resumed, "I am afraid we have thought too completely of just those little faults in her that were unpleasant to ourselves, and that, may be, we gave some cause for, too. And so we missed seeing really fine and noble things in her character that we must admire and love, too, if we would. And I tell you, girls, I often think how true it is what Auntie says, that when we once leave ourselves open to love for any one, and part with prejudice, it is wonderful what good we can see in them, and how the faults dwindle and dwindle, and how easy we find it to make excuses for those that remain. That is what Auntie says, and it seems true, doesn't it?"

"It condemns us pretty effectually, if it is," said Gertrude, who never shirked the legitimate conclusion of an argument, even when it told against herself. "I don't think any of us have laid ourselves very open to love Miss Langton, unless you, May, who can always see something good in every one."

"Oh, indeed, I have been in fault, too," said May, with genuine sweet humility. "You remember our lesson last Sunday, about love being the fulfilling of the law? Then it must be worse to fail in it than in anything else. Somehow that came into my mind when Miss Langton was speaking. No matter how obedient or studious we were, we had in a sort of way set ourselves against loving her. And, after all, girls, even if it was foolish for her to speak so, wasn't it a great compliment, too—a sort of appeal for our love? It wasn't temper made her say that, it seems to me, but a kind of lonely tender-heartedness."

"Well, May, you can make out the best case for anybody of any one I ever heard," said Emma. "But come, tell us your secret, for we must soon hurry home. Is it some penance for our sins?"

"Oh, no; not exactly," said May, coloring and laughing; "or if it is, I must do penance along with you. I am just as guilty, every bit. I do seem to preach dreadfully, girls, don't I? I wonder you don't all get tired of me—it's a good deal worse to preach than to be cross some times. So, now for the secret: You know next Tuesday is the first of May, and I thought we never could have a lovelier chance to show Miss Langton that we really did care more than she thought to have her back again. Suppose we all joined our purses together and made her a little present—a May basket would be the very thing. One of us could go real early and hang it upon the school-room door handle, so she would find it when she first came in. Let's every one put in a little nosegay, even if it was only a few violets, with our name to it; and let's choose a real pretty basket, one she would always like to use."

"That is just beautiful," they all declared in chorus. "What a sweet girl you are! It would be a May basket in more ways than one."

"We must give all the girls a chance to join; the more the merrier," cried Ada. "Only, it is a Secret Society, mind. And I wish we could hide some pretty little keepsake that would not fade, under the flowers."

"I saw the sweetest little blue and gold copy of Tennyson's 'May Queen' down town this morning; it wasn't very dear either—only two dollars." This suggestion came from Gertrude.

"Oh, that would be the very thing," said May, delightedly. "To-morrow's Thursday; we can speak about it among the other girls at recess; and then, the next day, we can bring all our dollars and cents, and elect two or three girls to go on Saturday and choose the basket and book; every one must get their flowers by themselves; and Monday evening you can all come round to Auntie's, and bring your flowers, and she will help us arrange them—she does such things so beautifully; and she will give us all a nice tea-party, too, I know. So be sure, every one, and ask their mother's leave in time."

"Oh, you may be sure of that," was the merry response. "We know what a lovely time there is when Aunt Grace asks us to spend an evening."

"What dear, good girls you are," said May, "to be so pleased with my plan; but I do think it will be just lovely."

"Yes, indeed, it will," Gertrude answered for the rest. "And Miss Morton will be pleased, too; she just loves to see people happy. And it's we that ought to thank you, May, for making us all better."

And then there were hurried adieus, for the afternoon was growing late; and they all sped home, full of delightful importance.

PART III.

It was wonderful what a softened atmosphere seemed to pervade that schoolroom during those intervening days. Their own altered frame of mind and purpose had invested their teacher with a novel and tender interest to the girls. It has been said that any crea-

ture—certainly any human creature—
whom we help becomes straightway more
or less dear to us; and so their meditated
kindness awoke an answering throb of gentleness and affection, and tolerance for her
whims, that all Miss Langton's really
faithful service might have failed to win.
The good seed of May's little lecture had
not dropped on stony ground; more than
one of her listeners pondered over it silently, seeing it illumined by the beauty
and sweetness of her own girlish example;
and could look back gratefully afterwards
to her influence as a help to purer and
nobler purpose both in thought and action.

Meanwhile, the wished-for May Day
dawned at last—a veritable morn of May;
even crowded city streets could not shut
out the radiant blue of the sky, or the fresh,
sweet breeze that *would* find its way, or the
song of a stray bird. Maria Langton
paused a moment, as she reached the school
house entrance, to drink in once again the
elixir of the air and rejoice in the glorious
sunshine. The tame monotony of her life
had not yet dulled her delight in Nature's
loveliness; and her heart, this morning,
was full of remembered spring-times, when

her happy, childish feet had lost themselves in daisy-sprinkled fields, and the violets and roses had made sweet the air around that early home. Even now, the perfumed breath of the woodlands seemed to visit her. She ascended the stairs so absorbed in thought that she did not notice, till she was close upon it, the blossom-laden basket, lightly covered by tissue-paper, which hung upon the handle of the door.

What could it mean?

She lifted it carefully and carried it into the empty school-room, her bewilderment giving place to an emotion too deep for expression as she removed the covering and saw, lying among that glowing, fragrant cluster of bouquets, this simple little card:

"The message of the May: to Miss Langton, from her loving pupils, in token of their joy at her recovery."

Her heart beat with an almost painful pressure; the tears rose welling to her eyes; she touched the flowers with reverent caressing fingers.

"And I doubted their love," she murmured. "I was jealous, and repined, and longed for another lot to be mine. O Lord, forgive my waywardness—make me more like the least of these thy little ones."

The great bell was clanging out its summons now; there were many feet echoing on the stairs; and girls, in shy clusters, stole quickly and silently into the room. Miss Langton sat behind her desk, with the basket on a small stand placed near her. Her face was very pale; but the girls thought they had never known what beautiful, soft, shining eyes she had until that moment.

"My dear, dear girls," she said, at last—and her voice had in it a new and exquisite thrill of happiness—"how can I thank you? I feel as if I had never deserved such sweet remembrance from you; but, indeed, you have made this one of the dearest days of my life. Will you each give me a kiss to complete it, and make me sure I am not dreaming?"

You may be certain the girls crowded round her and gave the caress with right good will. There was no distance between them now—never any more; whatever frailties of human intercourse might ruffle their companionship, the chill of reserve and dislike had melted away in the sunshine of heaven.

And was it not a curious and beautiful coincidence that when Miss Langton opened the New Testament to read the customary chapter for the day, before recitation began, that chapter should conclude with these immortal words:

"And now abideth Faith, Hope, Love, these three; but the greatest of these is Love."

And I ought to tell you, may be, that it was not until Miss Langton had her basket safe at home, and was placing the last of her floral darlings in its vase of cool water, that she found that dainty little book of blue and gold, which held the story of the poet's May Queen.

"HOME, SWEET HOME."

"As the bird to its sheltering nest
  When the storm on the hills is abroad,
So her spirit hath flown from this world of unrest,
  To repose on the bosom of God."

I WAS a passenger on the Pacific Coast steamship, Orizaba, from Port Harford to San Pedro, the port of Los Angeles. The vessel was crowded with tourists from San Francisco, and every state-room was full; so that those going on board, as I did, at an intermediate port, were fain to be content with sitting-room in the salon. The prospect of a whole day and night to be spent thus was rather appalling to one who knew from experience what it was to fall victim to all the horrors of sea-sickness; but, by great good fortune, I found refuge on one end of a lounge, whose only occupant for the moment was a kind-hearted little German woman; who, guessing from my forlorn aspect all the misery of dizziness and nausea, gathered herself and her belongings into the smallest possible compass, and invited me, in broken English and hospitable gestures, to lie down. Oh, the relief to drooping head and trembling limbs! I knew as long as I could shelter on that pillow I might bid defiance to my enemy; and lying there, after all, was really to be preferred to a berth in an isolated state-room, where one's only companions would be miserable fellow-sufferers. But here, in the cheerful salon, I could watch people coming and going, catch snatches of conversation, and amuse myself by trying to analyze the characters of those around me.

When the early autumn twilight darkened into sudden night, there was a general gathering in of all the promenaders from the decks, and talk and laughter filled the room. There was every variety of traveler from which to choose. Here was a rich lady from Denver, costly jewels in her ears and at her throat and sparkling on her white hand—a perfect sample of vain and foolish and vulgar display. Here was a tired mother with her three or four little ones—cross and sleepy, fain to slumber on the carpet at her feet; it was no pleasure trip to her, poor soul, but a wearisome "moving" from one town to another. Here was a school teacher coming back from her summer vacation, sunburned and happy. And in that far corner, hidden behind her long veil, sat a young widow with her baby girl asleep on her lap. Her husband had died a month ago, in the asylum for the insane at Napa—driven there by an overwhelming sense of pecuniary failure, caused by the dry season of the year before, which starved to death the flock of sheep on his Santa Barbara ranch. Now his wife and little daughter were returning to the ever open shelter of a father's and mother's home. There were types enough to furnish study for an idle observer through all the slowly passing hours.

The Denver lady atoned for her flaunting display of wealth by singing, delightfully, old ballads, when a young girl opened the piano and played the accompaniments. A lively discussion between the school-teacher and a visitor from the East, as to California's merits, followed, in which others soon joined. Two capitalists argued questions of finance; and two clergymen, creeds and education. So the night wore away, till those who had state-rooms withdrew; and the rest, disposed on chairs and lounges, and even on the floor, dropped into silence and sleep.

With the early morning, every one was on deck, ready for transfer to the "lighter" which was to bring us to the wharf. The sun was extremely hot, not a ripple on the glassy water, not a breath of wind; but the sea-sick sufferers found little respite from their misery in the heavy, oily odor of the "lighter's" machinery, and in the clouds of tobacco smoke which blew all about them from pipe and cigar as the passengers crowded together for an intermediate hour on the dirty, baggage-laden deck. For "first-class" travelers, the gentlemen of the party seemed to me singularly wanting in good manners and good feeling. I was growing ill almost to faintness by a cigar just behind me, when I caught sight of a lovely face a few feet distant. Its owner had been invisible the evening before, no doubt "enjoying the seclusion which a cabin grants"; and I gazed at her with a sudden interest and regret that there had been no chance for an acquaintance between us. Her large hazel eyes were full of liquid light, of love, and hope, and glad impatience; her beautiful red lips wore a smile of refined sweetness; her slight, graceful person was plainly clad in a neat traveling ulster; and her rich brown hair coiled smoothly beneath her hat. She looked the one ideal figure among that motley gathering. On the seat beside her she rested a heavy roll of music, firmly strapped together—too heavy a burden for her girlish hand or arm. I hoped to have had the chance of helping her, but the rush of the crowd to the gangplank when the, boat stopped, separated us still more, and I lost sight of her altogether.

There was the usual turmoil of seeing to trunks and baggage, for we were not granted the convenience of "checks," and then the passengers streamed into the waiting train. What was my surprise and pleasure, as I took the first available seat, to find its other occupant my lovely unknown! We soon fell into an entertaining chat about the incidents of the journey, and learned more or less of each other's personality. She was a music teacher—as I judged from her appearance, about twenty years of age—residing in a small town a few miles beyond my own destination. From some things she said, I gathered that she was the main dependence of a widowed mother, though a younger brother shared her labors by his cultivation of a few acres of vineyard belonging to their little home. She had been in San Francisco during a two months' vacation, perfecting herself in her profession by taking lessons from a celebrated pianist.

"My pupils are all eager to have me back again," she said smiling; "they think I ought to be as wonderful as Signor C— himself by this time. And just see what I am bringing them for exercise!" pointing to the roll of music. "There is thirty dollars of value bound up in that—all my summer's savings—but it will repay me well, I know."

I tried at her suggestion, but could hardly lift the heavy package.

"How did you carry it?" I exclaimed. "You should have sent it by express; it was not wise to fatigue yourself so."

"Oh, I did not feel it," she answered

brightly. "I could not bear to part with it —it is too precious—and I must play some of those airs for mamma to-night."

The day was very close and hot; the fine, sandy soil of the roads sifted in everywhere; the cars seemed to jolt unmercifully; the vineyards were brown and faded; the orange groves gray with dust; I was low-spirited and weary.

"How slow we seem to travel," I said; "this heat and noise give one a dreadful headache; did you ever hear such rumbling cars?"

"Oh," she answered, and her face lighted up with an angel's smile, "I can hear nothing but 'Home, Sweet Home.' It is all singing that to me; every bit of noise is like music. Only think how soon we shall be there!"

I felt rebuked by that sweet enthusiasm of affection. "I suppose your brother will meet you at the station?" I asked.

"Oh, yes; I know he will; if he is late what a shaking I will give him! But it will be a very loving shake," she added softly, and her eyes brightened with sudden tears.

She coughed slightly, now and then, as

she spoke—very slightly—and yet I turned to look at her now with a quick thrill of pain. Those large beautiful eyes, were they not too intensely luminous? That softly-moulded cheek, was it not growing thin, despite its rich color? And was there not a pathetic droop just faintly suggested by the perfect young form? And yet, such an atmosphere of youth and hope and love seemed to float around her, that these dark, vague misgivings shrank back ashamed.

Poor child! She turned to me, all unconscious of my mournful scrutiny, and held out a cordial hand in goodby as the whistle sounded for my station.

"Perhaps we shall meet again," she said kindly. "I hope you will find your friends well."

"And I hope the same for you," I replied, "and a happy meeting with those you love."

"Oh, it cannot help being that," she smiled; and as I caught a last glimpse of her face from the platform, as the cars rushed past me, the pure young lips seemed forming again their soft refrain of "Home, Sweet Home."

Many a time during the next four

months, when I was miles away from the place of our meeting, did I recall that lovely and loving face. It shone like a star amid other memories of the journey. The vulgar display of some, the supercilious haughtiness of others, the absolute unconsciousness of life's struggle among still more, of our wealthy travelers returning from their summer dissipations; and the hard, ungracious lines of worry and anxiety and eager striving stamped upon the faces of their less fortunate companions; were both alike thrown into vivid relief on the canvas of recollection by the memory of that picture of unselfish love and tender hope.

One day, I received, by chance, a copy of a paper published near her home; and among the notices of local events, I read the following: "Miss L— F— died last week of consumption. She had been ill several months, but grew rapidly worse after the death of her mother, which, as our readers will remember, took place about six weeks ago. She will be greatly lamented by her friends and pupils. She was but twenty-two years old." I laid the paper down, my eyes dim; yet my tears were not all of sorrow. Had not mother and child met once again, and forever, in "Home, Sweet Home"?

HER NEIGHBOR.

"But he, willing to justify himself, said unto Jesus, And who is my neighbor?"

"Love, which is sunlight of peace."

IF there was any one thing which gave Marianne Evans a special secret satisfaction, it was her name. Whether written or spoken—that is, if spoken correctly—it seemed to her the synonym of refinement and grace. She had never known the grandmother for love of whom it was bestowed; but in her mother's sitting-room hung an old-fashioned portrait—a fair young girl in the dress of sixty years ago; and Marianne had often sat looking at it, with eyes of absorbed fancy, while her mother recounted to her once again the old but ever new story of her grandmother's childhood and girlhood in that old cathedral town across the sea; of her marriage to the young captain of the good ship Dauntless; and that perilous voyage to the new world, with its stormy ending of shipwreck and rescue, which left her mother orphaned of a father's care. And then she had read, with all the sentimental sympathy of a girl of sixteen, Miss Austin's "Sense and Sensibility," missing, I fear, much of the author's real purpose, in her fervid interest in her lovely namesake of the tale.

Altogether, there seemed, to Marianne, to cling about the syllables of her name a halo of romantic association to which none of her companions' more commonplace titles could lay claim. It had given her a certain sense of pride and superiority, whenever she heard the roll called in school, that none but herself could answer to that name; and she felt a sort of pitying condescension for the Marthas and Elizas whose surnames were their only distinction from each other.

Alas! "pride must have a fall."

One September morning, when the school reassembled for the first time after vacation, there were two new pupils standing beside the teacher's desk, waiting till the seats should be apportioned.

I think I can see them still—those little twin-sisters—clinging timidly to one another, and looking with half-frightened eyes over the strange school-room. The poor, scanty dress told of a poverty-stricken home; and the cloud of soft, brown hair, wonderful in its luxuriance, that fell upon their shoulders, though brushed and tied back with a piece of faded ribbon, had evidently been the care of a hurried hand. But the large grey eyes and the broad, thoughtful foreheads of each, told of intellect—perhaps of genius—could it but be fostered into generous life. One felt an involuntary heartache at the thought of what narrow opportunities were theirs, at the thought of how little brightness or joy was possible to these young lives.

Marianne, in her fresh muslin robe, with her fair silken hair so carefully curled—the rounded contour and lovely bloom of her cheek telling so plainly of health and good food, and tender, watchful care of a happy and abundant home—formed a painful contrast. The other girls, too, though not types of such delicate beauty, nor all the children of homes so refined and wealthy as hers, yet happy, care-free, flourishing samples of youth, from homes of industry and comfort, unconscious of the real fret and strain of life—how pathetic was the contrast between their thoughtless light-heartedness and the look of constant, womanly anxiety that shadowed these young brows!

Marianne, and several of the older pupils, had dropped, as a matter of course, into their accustomed seats, and were busy arranging their books; the little bustle of apportioning uncertain or coveted desks was ended; and the tap of the bell brought sudden silence out of the subdued hum. Marianne looked around, to find that her nearest neighbors were the two little strangers, who, to their great relief and joy, had been allotted seats side by side. She felt an aggrieved disappointment that her own special "chum" was not there as usual; and perhaps she felt also a foolish and sinful contempt and repugnance at such close proximity to the poorest pupils in the school. But this was nothing to the secret rage and mortification that filled her heart when she listened to the calling of the roll and heard her unwelcome neighbors answer to the question of their names, "Mary Fraser, ma'am," and "Anne Fraser, ma'am."

A look of amused intelligence passed from face to face over he school-room. School-girls are proverbially quick-witted, and Marianne's weakness about her name was no secret to her mates. If they did not disguise a rather ungenerous sense of the ridiculous in this unexpected parody of her cherished title, she really could blame no one but herself; for it was not in girl nature not to resent her assumption of a "peculiar inherited grace," even about a name. But though the deepened flush on her cheek betrayed her consciousness of what was passing, pride came to her rescue, and she responded "present," when her own name followed, with clear, unfaltering distinctness. Her self-control silenced a half-suppressed titter before it reached the teacher's ears; and even when the bell rang for recess, and laughter and talk took the place of decorum, whatever comments the girls might pass among themselves, there were none so bold just yet as openly to assail Marianne.

The little sisters did not venture forth among the chattering crowd, but remained at their desks, grateful to be unobserved and forgotten by the rest, talking in low tones to one another over their lessons.

There were other surprises in store, for all the school, as well as Marianne. When the classes came to be organized, it was found, to the general astonishment, that in grammar, and history, and reading, Mary and Anne Fraser, in spite of their thirteen years, easily took front rank with those much older; though, in arithmetic and algebra, they fell behind; and Marianne had the renewed mortification of finding herself in unexpected close companionship, even in her favorite studies, with these presumptuous waifs of fortune.

When little Mary stood up to read Mrs. Hemans' "Landing of the Pilgrims," she seemed to forget her usual timidity in the inspiration of the poet, and the words rang with new music as they thrilled through her clear young voice; all the constraint and anxiety vanished for the moment from her face; while her twin-sister regarded her with the absorbed enthusiasm of affection. It was a beautiful and unique spectacle, and something of its beauty and pathos forced its way even to Marianne's reluctant heart.

"They are the most extraordinary children!" she cried in a half-provoked tone to Miss Morton—whose path lay, for some distance, in a direction with her own—as they were walking home that evening.

Somehow she could speak to her teacher when she shrank from facing the half-sarcastic comments of the girls. Dear Miss Morton! whose wise, loving touch was always bringing harmony out of discord—how many young lives had cause to bless her influence!

"Yes," she answered now, "they are remarkably intelligent, but I do not wonder they are so, for their childhood has had careful training. Poor little things! I fear their chief dependence now must be on what they can learn at school."

"Do you know any thing of them then?" asked Marianne, with keen curiosity.

"Yes; their mother was a school-mate of my own; married when she was only seventeen—a very happy marriage, too, I believe. Her husband was a young clergyman, devoted to his calling, and highly educated.

I was at their home once, about five years ago, and even then one could plainly see the uncommon care and interest both he and his wife took in the training of their children. Poor little ones! it is a sad change for them, from their happy childhood of learning and play in that quiet old village to this narrow city life."

"They are orphans, I suppose?" asked Marianne, in a softened voice.

"Yes, their father and mother both died about two years ago—victims of some epidemic prevailing at the time. They left but small means, and the two little girls fell to the care of a widowed aunt, who had no children of her own. She had been a teacher of drawing, but these dull times reduced her number of pupils so seriously that she was compelled to remove to the city in the hope of obtaining more employment. Of course, being a stranger and without influence, she has had a hard struggle, and is glad to eke out the earnings of her profession by taking in sewing. I have been thinking of calling on your mamma, to give her Mrs. Morris's address; perhaps she might have something for her to do."

"I am sure she would," said Marianne. "Mamma would be quite interested in the children, I know."

She almost felt shamed out of her own prejudice and dislike by Miss Morton's recital; and thought, as they parted company and she pursued her way alone, how grieved her mother would be, did she know the temper of her mind that day.

But while she did not exactly "let the sun go down" upon her wrath, I am afraid it rose with fresh vigor beneath his morning beam; and her reflections were anything but gracious as she took her seat again beside her obnoxious school-mates.

PART II.

Such studious little creatures as these twin-sisters were! Surely Miss Morton had never had such earnest, willing pupils before! It was almost painful to witness their eagerness; and Miss Morton felt herself that she must call a halt to such persistent industry, and insist on their sharing the play and fresh air of recess.

"Mary and Anne," she said one day, as she tapped the bell for the welcome signal, and the girls scattered like a flock of birds, "come to the desk, my dears; I wish to speak to you."

The children came up to her, hand in hand.

"Now, my dearest little girls," she went on, "I can not praise you enough for your obedience and attention in all your lessons; but there is one thing I must find fault with, and cannot allow any longer. You must not stay in doors at recess. Run out with the other girls, and breathe the fresh air and have a good romp."

"But, please, Miss Morton, we can study so well at recess; and we want so much to get on fast, and come to be teachers, so we can help dear auntie."

What anxious little faces they were!

"You will study all the better, dears, and come on all the faster, by taking a little breathing spell. All work and no play makes a dull girl as well as a dull boy; so run out now, and get better acquainted with the girls, and let me see some roses in these pale cheeks."

It was a hard ordeal for the timid twins to venture among that laughing, active crowd; but the first trial over, they soon began to win friendly regard, and the sweet childlike mirth, that had been so sadly shadowed by grief and poverty, began to bubble up from its pure well-spring of love and happiness. Their gentleness and refinement, and bright intelligence and unselfish readiness to join in whatever gave pleasure to the rest, could not fail to win a way, and they had soon more than one warm, special friend eager to take their part. Marianne herself felt the influence; but she could not forgive the accident of their names, nor their unconscious rivalry of her position as the "clever pupil" of the school.

"I wonder how you can help loving Mary and Anne," Jenny Seaton said to her, with the audacious freedom for which she was renowned. "Are you jealous, Marianne? Or aren't you willing anybody should even halve your name? For my part, I think it is much prettier divided between those sweet little creatures, than to belong entirely to such a proud thing as you." And she ran off with a mocking laugh, before Marianne could collect herself to answer.

"Did you ever hear such a good composition as Mary Fraser's," one of the elder girls was saying one Friday afternoon, as they loitered in groups after school was "out." "So simple and natural; not a bit like a set composition. She made me feel as if I could just see the woods and the village, and the old farmhouse. Dear! if I could only transform my wooden essays into stuff like that!" And Eliza Green gave a comical sigh.

Above all the names she knew, Marianne had always regarded this unfortunate combination with supreme contempt; yet something stirred in her heart now like admiration for this plain girl with her plainer name. Was it not possible that even the most plebeian name might become the synonym for love and grace, if worn by such a generous spirit?

"But what did you think of Anne's poem?" struck in the irrepressible Jenny. "There was a surprise for you! Real poetry, too, though only a child's song. Even Miss Morton did not expect that, though she thinks so much of them both. None of the rest of us could compete there, I think, even if we tried. What makes you so silent, Marianne? Poets are born, not made, you know—no use to be jealous of them." And she broke into a ringing laugh.

"You have no right to accuse me of jealousy," Marianne answered, coldly; "but I must confess, whatever merit Anne's poem may have, I do not see the use or wisdom of encouraging her in such efforts; what good can it ever do her in a working life?"

"Oh, as for that, begging your pardon, my lady, all our lives should be working ones, as your own dear mother told us in Sunday school last week. And in the next place, the nest may be very ragged and small, but that won't keep the bird from singing when the music is in its breast. Genius is always vindicating democracy."

"Oh, girls," broke in Martha Lane, "do you remember that horrible 'pome' last year—when that hateful Luvia Roberts, who was always telling us of her father's money and servants, saw fit to invoke the muse?"

And at this recollection the whole group joined in contagious laughter, even Marianne's reserve giving way.

"I know that 'pome' by heart to-day," said Jennie; "now I have learned Anne's, too; I want to recite it to mamma when I get home. They make two good companion pieces, don't they? One might label them Vulgarity and Nature."

"I shouldn't wonder if Mary or Anne won the prize at the next examination," said Eliza. "That would be a new departure—to see it carried off by the youngest pupil in school."

Marianne gave an unconscious start. She had won the prize last year, and was particularly anxious not to fail now. Her father, who took great pride in her attainments, had promised a trip to Niagara to celebrate her success. She grew actually pale at the bare thought of failure.

"Look to your laurels, Marianne!" cried the mischievous Jenny, whose quick eye had noticed her involuntary perturbation. And with this parting shot, their paths separated.

PART III.

Marianne's father and mother, though wealthy, were by no means slavish imitators of their more fashionable acquaintances. They had a wholesome, old-fashioned, democratic faith in the virtue of the free school as a sphere for developing character, for cultivating independence of thought and respect for the rights of others. I cannot say that their daughter fully agreed in this view. She had often looked longingly after some of her girl friends who attended "select" young ladies' academies; but especially envied those who pursued their education in the shadow of the convent. It seemed to Marianne the acme of exclusive refinement to pass behind those high walls, to walk in those old gardens, and to study under the mild and saintly rule of the good Sisters. It was a little bit of mediaeval romance still left to flourish undisturbed in our bustling nineteenth century. She had even ventured an appeal to her father on the subject, but met with a very decided, though kind, refusal.

"No, no, my dear," he said; "we are not living in the middle ages now, and it is not healthy to breathe their atmosphere any more than any dead air. We must be true sons and daughters of our own era, if we would fill our place worthily; and to gain wisdom from the past, it is not necessary to turn our back on the present. In the free school, you meet with boys and girls from all conditions of life; and, as a rule, the teachers are, like Miss Morton, faithful and conscientious, without showing respect of persons. Whether you realize it now or not, the effect upon your womanhood must be elevating—in giving you broad and just views of our relations to others as men and women, and as citizens of a common country. No, I have too much faith in the promise of my Marianne's head and heart, despite the foolish little notions she has allowed to creep into her brain at present, to narrow her by an exclusive contact with companions, however pleasing or well-behaved, who have never seen below the surface of their own particular set."

"But, papa, you would not intend my

education to close with the free school? I will be through with that this term."

"Certainly not, my dear. I hope you will pass so good an examination that you will be promoted immediately to the high school; and after your graduation from it, I would like to give you a few years at Vassar, or some institution of equal standing. Then with your natural gifts you will be really an accomplished, and a genuinely intellectual woman, able to grasp, for yourself, the true aspects of life. While, if you had been confined to the narrow limits of a convent or young ladies' seminary, I fear the result would be very different."

On the whole, Marianne retired from this talk somewhat comforted. Her own native good sense, when she allowed it fair play, could not but acknowledge the justness of her father's reasoning; and as she thought of the generous future of growth and purpose which her parents' love had planned, she recalled for a moment, with softened sympathy, the narrow horizon life revealed to the little twin-sisters.

"And they *have* genius," her heart whispered. "Jenny was right. I may be clever and learned, perhaps, after a while, but I haven't *that*. Why it doesn't seem fair— it is cruel— to think they should be shut off from everything, and that I should have so much."

A flush of conscious shame mounted to her brow.

"I suppose I *have* been jealous," she thought. "But then, I do hate to lose the prize, and that lovely journey papa has promised. And if they only had different names! It is odious to have one's name mimicked like that."

However, she was a little less icy in her manner, next day at school, and the timid and surprised response of her namesakes touched a chord in her heart. The thaw had begun, though the surface crust as yet showed but faint token of its progress; but the sunshine of love was brightening toward spring, and however fleeting clouds might chill its warmth, the frost must melt daily, more and more, till the flowers of sweet good-nature appear, and the singing birds of sisterly help and affection make glad the day.

Autumn had given place to winter, and winter was melting into spring. It only wanted two weeks of the dreaded, yet haven't *that*. Why it doesn't seem fair— it is cruel— to think they should be shut off from everything, and that I should have so much."

A flush of conscious shame mounted to her brow.

"I suppose I *have* been jealous," she thought. "But then, I do hate to lose the prize, and that lovely journey papa has promised. And if they only had different names! It is odious to have one's name mimicked like that."

However, she was a little less icy in her manner, next day at school, and the timid and surprised response of her namesakes touched a chord in her heart. The thaw had begun, though the surface crust as yet showed but faint token of its progress; but the sunshine of love was brightening toward spring, and however fleeting clouds might chill its warmth, the frost must melt daily, more and more, till the flowers of sweet good-nature appear, and the singing birds of sisterly help and affection make glad the day.

Autumn had given place to winter, and winter was melting into spring. It only wanted two weeks of the dreaded, yet education to close with the free school? I will be through with that this term."

"Certainly not, my dear. I hope you will pass so good an examination that you will be promoted immediately to the high school; and after your graduation from it, I would like to give you a few years at Vassar, or some institution of equal standing. Then with your natural gifts you will be really an accomplished, and a genuinely intellectual woman, able to grasp, for yourself, the true aspects of life. While, if you had been confined to the narrow limits of a convent or young ladies' seminary, I fear the result would be very different."

On the whole, Marianne retired from this talk somewhat comforted. Her own native good sense, when she allowed it fair play, could not but acknowledge the justness of her father's reasoning; and as she thought of the generous future of growth and purpose which her parents' love had planned, she recalled for a moment, with softened sympathy, the narrow horizon life revealed to the little twin-sisters.

"And they *have* genius," her heart whispered. "Jenny was right. I may be clever and learned, perhaps, after a while, but I wished-for, examination day, when, one March morning, there was a sensation in Miss Morton's school-room. For the first time since Mary and Anne Fraser had entered there, one of the twins appeared without her mate. "Something is wrong," was the general surmise, as a murmur of surprise ran round the room; and when Miss Morton announced that Mary was seriously ill with a cold which threatened pneumonia, there were no eyes which did not glance with kind sympathy at the quivering lip and tearful face of poor little Anne.

"Her aunt has allowed me to take Anne to my own home for a time, till any fear of contagion is past," Miss Morton explained. "So your parents need not feel any alarm. I hope you will remember to tell them this. And now we will proceed with lessons."

"So there is one out of the running," said Jenny Seaton, at recess. "I haven't any hope of the prize, myself; though I mean to try my best. But there is no doubt of you, Marianne, unless Anne Fraser beats you. Any way, you have one rival less, now."

"I would rather have the two," said Marianne, truthfully; "there is no triumph in outshining the absent. But I might not win, any way. I am not so vain as to think none of the other girls can excel me."

"Oh, we all know well enough you are 'the wittiest,' as well as 'the prettiest,'" answered Jenny. "If you weren't so proud, Marianne, you might be 'the one we love best.' Aren't you sorry, now, you felt so jealous of those poor little things' names? I think it is dreadfully lonesome to hear Anne answer the roll alone."

"I couldn't coax her out at all," said Martha Lane. "She has no heart for anything but her books; she seems to be studying for Mary as well as herself."

"I hope she will win the prize with all my heart," said Eliza Green. "I'd rather, a great deal than get it myself. Though I've so little chance, it doesn't take much generosity for me to say that," she added, laughing.

Marianne had walked apart, but her ear caught the last words. Could she echo them? She dared not answer, yes. Yet she felt sincerely grieved for the illness of her little school-fellow; she hoped earnestly that it might not prove serious. But to give up the coveted prize?—to be willing and glad to give it up to brighten those meager young lives?

"Why, they are only thirteen," she argued inly; "it is really absurd to suppose they could carry it off from others so much older. And they may win plenty of prizes before they leave school; but for me to miss this last one!—how it would disappoint papa and mamma! And then that trip to Niagara, I have set my heart on."

Yet her heart and conscience were ill at ease. To quiet their reproaches, she showed more than usual kindness and interest in her manner to Anne, whose sorrowful little soul gratefully responded; but Marianne knew that such kindness was but a subterfuge—that she did not love her neighbor as herself.

Her mention of Mary's illness roused her mother's sympathy at once, and she hastened to call on Mrs. Morris, and carry what cheer and comfort she could to the poor little sufferer.

Marianne listened with troubled interest to her mother's report, after each frequent visit.

"I cannot let you go with me yet, my dear," Mrs. Evans said, a week later; "Mary is still very ill, but the doctor thinks it may not now prove a dangerous fever. Her little sister, even, is not allowed to see her. But after school closes, when I hope she will be fairly better, I shall be glad to take you. We may learn many a lesson, child, from adversity bravely borne; and though my business intercourse with Mrs. Morris proved to me that she was both a capable and intelligent woman, my actual knowledge of her home life, in its humble surrounding, has won my highest regard. There is no lady I know more worthy of admiration, in the refinement and culture of her mind; and her little niece is a proof, even as a child, of the pure, moral atmosphere of her home. It really humbles me to witness the faith, and courage, and tender love of that good aunt, pressed, as she is, on every side, by care and anxiety and toil; and then to come back to our own delightful home, and remember how often I have allowed the veriest trifles to fret me!"

"Oh, mamma, if I could only be half as good as you!" exclaimed Marianne; and then she stopped, with a sudden, shocked sense of what her mother's judgment would be on the foolish pride and ungenerous selfishness which had closed her heart against her gentle little school-mates.

"If mamma can feel like that," she thought, "how willing I ought to be for those poor girls to have that one little triumph and joy to make them glad. How ashamed I ought to be when I look around on all the beautiful things papa and mamma are always giving me, to think that I cannot bear to lose this one little thing that might be theirs."

PART IV.

The eventful day had dawned at last. The school-room was crowded with unwonted visitors—proud and anxious parents and grave Directors. From among the throng of bright young faces, fronting the teacher's platform, only one was absent—poor little Mary was still held a prisoner by illness, though the happy light in Anne's eyes and the glad, kindly murmur of sympathy among the girls would have told you at once that all danger was past, and that a few weeks would see the sisters together again.

There were three prizes to be awarded: one for geography—a beautiful globe, the gift of Marianne's mother; one for arithmetic—a rosewood writing desk, from one of the directors; and one for composition and rhetoric. In this last prize, the excitement and interest of the school culminated. It was from a gentleman who desired his name to remain unknown, and the prize itself was to remain a secret until the award was made. Like true daughters of Eve, the unknown good was the one most eagerly desired; and though they gave absorbed attention, and acquitted themselves to the best of their ability in all the preceding exercises, yet the electric flushing and paling of every cheek, when the concluding act was reached, showed where the girlish heart was most enlisted.

The examination in rhetoric came to a creditable close; and then each girl, in order of her seniority, rose to read her essay, as her name was called. Marianne was first; her subject was "Peace"; it was beautifully and vigorously expressed, though perhaps some passages were just a trifle grandiloquent; but it showed fine command of language, and a thoughtful and cultivated mind. The other girls followed in rotation, with subjects as various as the writers; but all doing credit, more or less pronounced, to the instruction of their teacher and their own application.

Last of all the list came Anne Fraser. Such a tiny figure she looked as she rose in her place; for the girls had not been grouped on the platform, like more ambitious *debutantes* (that distinction was reserved for high-school and college), but each stood simply at her accustomed desk. To Miss Morton's eyes, there was a touch of genuine pathos in that picture of the child forced for once out of her shy seclusion, and facing such an ordeal without her darling mate. Her simple frock of black and white calico was in striking contrast to some of the ruffled and dainty lawn dresses beside her; but the delicately-moulded form; the sweet, pure face, its pallor tinged now by a sensitive flush; the large, serious grey eyes, and broad calm forehead, shadowed by that cloud of soft, brown hair, made up a lovely portrait that needed no extraneous aid of dress or ornament to win sympathy and favor. Just at first, the low voice faltered, but soon, forgetting herself in the recall of the feeling that had inspired her writing, her tones rose clear and full, with childlike fervor of recollection. She had not drawn on any store of youthful learning, but from the well-spring of a child's sweet love and memory, and "A Day in our Old Home" touched every listener with the impulse and innocence of their own dawning. Just so blue had the skies bent above them in that old time; just so had the breezes thrilled every nerve; just so fresh and pure had the flowers bloomed; the sparkling streams had flowed; and the happy birds had sung just so in the branching trees. There was more than one eye wet with unconscious tears when the clear voice ceased; for a child's soft touch had swept away for a little while the clouding cares and ambitions of life; and back into those green pastures and beside those still and crystal waters, a child's hand had led the way.

There was a little outburst of applause that wakened Anne to a half-frightened consciousness again; and with a timid bow, she was glad to take refuge in her seat.

Music and singing occupied the interval, during which the committee made their decision; and then came the award. It had been a difficult and delicate task to decide fairly in a school where all the pupils reached such a high-water mark of average excellence; but, at last, the prize for geography was awarded to Jenny Seaton; for arithmetic, to Martha Lane.

Marianne heard these verdicts with comparative indifference; it was the mysterious third prize on which her heart was set; but the delight of Jenny and Martha was overflowing and unconcealed; nor did their school-fellows fail in generous congratulation when the first brief pang of disappointment had passed. Though the majority had entered the lists in competition for the third prize, it had been tacitly felt and acknowledged by all that the only real rivalry lay between Marianne and Anne; and the whole school was quivering with suppressed excitement now. But dear little Anne, while she shared in the general interest, was really quite unconscious of her special part in the drama. She had written her simple essay as the birds sing—from the spontaneous overflow of a loving and poetic nature—delighting in the song for the song's sake; but to actually compete with an accomplished young lady like Marianne—whom the bashfulness of thirteen regarded with admiring awe—was beyond her wildest ambition. And so, when the committee announced their decision, and she heard "the prize for composition awarded to Anne Fraser," the room seemed to spin round and round the little victor, and all the crowd of people to mingle in a bewildered haze. But it was really true! She could hear one of the Directors explaining that while all the essays showed unusual care and thought, there were two distinguished especially by originality and beauty of style; and that the final choice had to be made between these. Miss Evans' "Peace" showed a range of thought and reading admirable in a young girl, and the language chosen was chaste and forcible; but Miss Fraser's "Day in Our Old Home," though dealing with a less pretentious theme, and admitting of less research and illustration, had yet shown such a natural and just observation of daily sights and sounds, such a close sympathy with the varying aspects of nature, and so playful and tender a fancy, that the committee, judging as impartially as possible, had decided unanimously that the prize should be hers. And, then, amid a great tempest of applause, Miss Morton came forward, bearing a beautiful little statuette of Hope—an exquisite little terra-cotta figure, whose every curve and line, from the lightly poised foot to the graceful head, was an inspiration of loveliness and joy.

Whatever their faults, girls are, as a rule, generous creatures, and there were but few in that throng who envied Anne a gift which every girlish heart recognized as peculiarly dear to itself. As for her, poor child!—blushing, trembling, altogether overwhelmed with this miraculous triumph—she came forward to receive the prize. The downcast eyes were raised in sudden brave acknowledgment, as her teacher's loving approval was seconded by the ladies and gentlemen grouped around her, and by the renewed cheering of her comrades; but the quivering lips could not frame a word. More than one mother dropped a furtive tear, as she gazed at the little orphan in her simple garb; and more than one among those dignified Directors felt his father's heart thrill with tender sympathy.

And so it was all over; and from amid a throng of kisses and congratulations Anne escaped, to bear her treasure home.

PART V.

"My dear," said Mrs. Evans to her daughter about two weeks later, "I am going to see Mrs. Morris to-day about some sewing, and I wish you would come with me. As vacation is not over yet, Anne and Mary will be at home, and your visit will please them. Mary is quite well now, I believe, and I think it a pity to leave you alone at home all the afternoon."

"Yes, mamma," said Marianne, with some embarrassment, "I will get ready at once." She did not utter her secret thought that this visit boded no particular pleasure either to her or her hostesses.

"Why in the world should they care to see me?" she reflected while dressing. "I have never done anything to make them care; and it has all been a humiliation for me."

But her mother had a purpose in this visit, unknown to her. She had watched with secret anxiety the proud patience with which Marianne had borne her defeat; and grieved that the noble and generous impulses of her child's nature had not yet vanquished her wounded self-esteem.

As for Marianne herself, she had been unhappy and at war with her own heart ever since that unlucky examination. The disappointment of her promised journey was a very deep one; but deeper still was the sense of her father's disappointment in her failure. Though he had said, with cheery good humor:

"Never mind, daughter; Niagara will keep; there are other examinations looming in the future, and your essay was good enough to satisfy any reasonable father." Yet she could not reconcile herself to this consoling tenderness, in place of the proud caress and reward of her success. Her mother, she felt instinctively, cared most of all for the just and generous temper of mind which could accept either failure or success without injury to moral feeling; but though she knew the spirit in which she had met this trial was a daily grief to that loving and clear-sighted judge, she could not yet school her mind to a true submission, nor open her heart to gentler, happier influences.

It was a scene of peaceful industry on which the door opened, when Marianne and her mother reached Mrs. Morris' lodging. The whirr of the sewing machine was interrupted at sound of their knock, and the little sisters raised their heads from earnest study over a book, as their aunt admitted the visitors. Marianne was struck, as her mother had been, by the courtesy and refinement of Mrs. Morris' manner; and by the tokens, poor though the room was in furnishing and size, of the intelligence and culture of the indwellers of this humble home. The little walnut cabinet, with its precious store of books; the writing desk in the corner; the one or two engravings on the wall; the box of mignonette on the window-sill, were all reminders of the happier, freer life to which they had belonged; and witnesses of the brave and loyal endeavor that sought through toil and stress to keep still strong and unpolluted the highest cravings of the young souls committed to its charge.

Marianne felt how unworthy her sense of mortification and defeat had been, as she entered this atmosphere, and honestly tried to return with cordial frankness the twins' timid but delighted greeting. But timid though she was, Mary was too full of the joy of her loving little heart in her sister's triumph to resist this opportunity of displaying it; and while Anne hung shyly back, she seized Marianne's hand, and, all unconscious of the hidden turmoil and contest the prize had caused, drew her forward to their own special nook beside the window. There, in a small recess in the wall, like a patron saint in a niche, stood the little statuette; the wall behind it and the shelf on which it rested covered with cloth of rich deep blue (the remnants, to tell the truth, of pretty cloaks long since worn out). The gilt-headed nails, tacking the cloth, were studded here and there like stars; while round the base of the figure little clusters of spring flowers—violets and daisies, gathered by the children from the common near by—were scattered in lovely disarray, like a votive offering before a shrine. The warm afternoon sunshine streamed in at the window, transfiguring in its radiant glow the artist's dream of Hope, and the two young faces that gazed on it with rapt delight in its significant beauty.

And as she looked, the warm sunlight of sympathy stole into Marianne's heart. All her foolish prejudice and pride and wounded vanity seemed to melt away; she heard once more the angel-message of "peace, good will," and the soft echo of her Master's words, "Love thy neighbor as thyself."

"We never could have dreamed of such a thing!" Anne's voice was saying, in shy depreciation of winning such a treasure; "neither Mary nor I had the least hope."

"And now you have Hope herself," said Marianne, with such a sweet ring in her laugh that her mother turned to listen, with sudden conviction that the clouds had cleared away.

"And it was such a surprise for dear auntie!" they both exclaimed together.

"Oh, we were so happy, that day!—to think that Mary had got well—and this to happen, too!" And Anne ended with a sigh of exquisite content.

"Not one of us deserved it half so well," said Marianne, kissing the pretty mouth; "and I am sure none of us could have taken such pleasure in it, or known how to place it so beautifully. I am glad, with all my heart, you won it Anne—for Mary's sake, too. You see, it could not have been a doubled prize to any of the rest of us—we have only one pair of twins."

"Isn't she lovely, auntie?" the little girls cried, when Marianne and her mother had gone.

"I used to think her proud," said Mary; "but she isn't really, a bit. She seemed more pleased for Anne to win Hope than herself. I would do any thing for her."

What sweet and tender confidence, what confession of fault, what wise and loving encouragement for the future, passed between mother and daughter in their quiet half hour that evening at bed-time, we will not detail; but to father and mother, and friends and school-mates, a sweet humility seemed henceforth to blend with Marianne's sprightly wit and genuine love of knowledge; an ever-growing, ever-deepening sense of oneness with the lives around her, that made her truly, in spirit, "look not only on her own things, but also on the things of others."

With what different feelings did she welcome back her once obnoxious schoolmates to their seats beside her own, when vacation was ended. How soon the mysterious influence of love and hope bestowed on these little ones bound her heart to them! How soon even the once detested echo of their names sounded like the echo of their sweet child-affection only, recalling, like a fading dream, her own past folly!

And when, the following year, she passed with honor to the wider sphere of the high school, and her father, kissing her in proud congratulation, said in playful earnest, "Ask what you will, Queen Esther, even to the half of my kingdom!" Marianne, with one swift glance at her mother, buried her face on his shoulder, and said, with a sob he hardly understood:

"Oh, papa, may I, really? Then, do you remember Niagara? And may I have Mary and Anne Fraser to go along with us?"

"Those two nice little girls I saw in

school? Oh, I remember—one of them carried off the prize last year.

"Well, you are a tender-hearted little queen, and the king must be true to his word. You had better get the trio ready, mamma; and send the bills to me. What are you crying for, puss?"

BROKEN PROMISES.

" When the morning came, the village awoke.

" The mowers betook themselves to the meadows, the children to school; the larks, singing deliriously, rose into the light of the beautiful sun.

" On earth there was nothing changed, only a mother that wept."

WHAT a charming woman Mrs. Dillon is!" said Isabel, closing the door after their visitor's leave-taking. "So kind and winning, and so pretty!"

"When did you ever fall in love with virtue that had not beauty to recommend it?" laughed practical Jenny. "I am willing to believe all good of our new friend; but trust me, Bella, hearts as tender beat beneath the gown of serge as under silken robe, and eyes as gentle beam from homelier faces."

"Ah, well, Jenny, she will learn wisdom soon enough," said mamma, with fond indulgence for the enthusiasm of seventeen years, while a half-sigh gave reluctant assent to the truth of her eldest daughter's words. "I envy that early belief still—that goodness and beauty cannot live apart."

"No, indeed," broke in impulsive Isabel; "and I am sure, Jenny, it is a thousand times more delightful to think of Blossom driving out with such a sweet, bright, merry-hearted companion as Mrs. Dillon than with some prim old maid or lecturing matron, no matter how good they were. Isn't she good, Clari?" she added, turning to a girl perhaps four years her senior, who had remained silent hitherto.

"I hope so," she said, smiling gravely, "I would not think any one good who could disappoint faith like yours, dear Bella."

"But you knew Mrs. Dillon before she came to live here; and aren't you proud to have her for a friend—don't you love her? Ah, I am sure you must love her dearly! I am sure my whole heart went out to her when she asked mamma's leave to take Blossom to the flower-show. Such kindnesses must be common acts with her, for why should we be her special favorites?"

"She has the great happiness of possessing the means of giving pleasure to others," replied Clarinda, evasively; her tone was troubled, as if there was some slight conflict passing in her mind, and Jenny's searching glance confused her self-possession. She tied her bonnet-strings a little hurriedly, and rose to go.

"I have stayed too long," she said, "and aunt will be waiting tea. Good-by, Mrs. Maurice; good-by, Jenny. I will be at the church at four to-morrow, Bella. Good-by, sweet Blossom!" and she bent to kiss a little girl reclining on a couch near the window.

You would never have guessed, if it had not been told you, that this wan little creature, crippled and helpless, this poor blighted flower of childhood, could be the wearer of so fair a name. Yet she had been a perfect blossom once, as lovely in her infant beauty as any of the fairest blooms of May; and mother and sisters, remembering the rosy cheek, and dimpled chin, and rounded limbs, and all the glad, unconscious mirth and baby graces of their darling, clung fondly still to the name bestowed in loving pride, and dearer now for mournful recollection.

"Poor little thing," thought Clarinda Ross, as she went down the street. "No, she dare not disappoint her; it would be too, too cruel; she is not so heartless as that!"

At that moment Mrs. Dillon, the object of her doubting indignation, swept past in her chariot, bowing and smiling as she caught the young girl's glance. Would she have been as gracious had she known her secret thought? Yet she had an instinctive sense that with Clarinda she had been weighed in the balances and found wanting. There was an unacknowledged, tacit feeling of repulsion on either side, the withdrawal of earnest conviction from frivolous assent—of truth unsullied from honor lightly held and lightly forfeited. The brilliant woman of the world shrank before the clear judgment and keen insight of the young orphan girl, poor and unknown; the favorite of fortune, admired and caressed, coveted the homage of the village music teacher more than that of all the gay throng that followed her steps—coveted an approval which she knew no mere glitter of success, no meretricious qualities, could ever claim.

Mrs. Dillon had two grand aims constantly before her; one was to shine in society; the other to be quoted and praised as a "Lady Bountiful," a dispenser of elegant charities. No vulgar cases of distress could claim her pity, no fingers coarse with toil receive the alms dropped from her soft white palm. Some softening halo of romance, or interesting grief, must veil the harsher aspects of any poverty on which her gaze might dwell. Yet, though Clarinda, familiar with the real trials and temptations which beset the poor, could have no sympathy with this dainty and delicate Christian beneficence, she had early discovered in Mrs. Dillon's character a flaw still more serious than this fastidious nicety of charitable impulse.

Their acquaintance had begun under circumstances peculiarly pleasing to the sensitive soul of the lady. A night of storm and rain; a young girl, pale and breathless, standing at the open door, shading her eyes from the dazzling light of the gas jet; the shawl, hastily thrown over head, falling back from a slim graceful figure; the rich brown hair above her brow damp with moisture; the small hand nervously holding the handle of the door. It was like a scene from a story book—all the accessories were most charming; and happy indeed was Mrs. Dillon to render what graceful attention she could, in a case which so satisfied her esthetic requirements. It had all originated in a very natural mistake on Clarinda's part; the aunt with whom she lived, who supplied as far as might be the place of parents dying too early for their child to understand her loss, had been very ill with a tedious and dangerous fever, but, after weeks of suffering, was at last pronounced convalescent. On the night in question, she had alarmed her niece by a sudden fainting fit, and no effort of Clarinda's could rouse her from the deathly stupor. The doctor who attended Mrs. Ross lived just across the street, and, leaving the lamp alight, Clarinda hurried out to seek him, but, confused by the darkness and her own agitation, she mistook the house and rang at Mrs. Dillon's door instead. The sound of her sweet, eager voice in parley with the servant reached the ear of the lady through the open parlor door, and drew her irresistibly to the presence of the speaker. It must be confessed that Clarinda was exceedingly touched by her new friend's kindness that night. She still recalled it with a pang of grateful tenderness; but, alas, alas, how soon was the fine gold dimmed!

Mrs. Dillon sent a servant for the doctor at once, allowing Clarinda to run back to her aunt; and following herself, through the mist and rain, accompanied by a maid, bearing many little comforts and luxuries for the invalid. The immediate occasion for her services passed, she did not withdraw her friendship, but became daily apparently more attached to Clarinda. Mrs. Ross was naturally delighted by the intimacy. And Clarinda—ah! was it not natural that she should welcome this sweet variation in the dull routine of her life? These rooms, so small and poorly furnished, how they seemed to expand and brighten and lose that conscious air of poverty when Mrs. Dillon's lovely face peeped in at the open door, and Mrs. Dillon's clear voice asked, "Is Clari here?" How pleasant it was, coming home—oh, so weary!—on Saturday night, from the endless struggle with dull pupils and unreasonable employers, to hear her aunt say as she poured out the tea, "There is a note for you, Clari. Mrs. Dillon will call for you to-morrow afternoon; it is her Sunday for visiting the orphan school; and the drive will do you good."

No doubt, the drive did do her good, with such a sweet companion; so did the sight of the little homeless waifs, sheltered by charity. Her eye beamed with sympathy as she looked over the throng of young, eager faces—some rosy with health, some pale with recent illness, some timid and shrinking, some confidently gay—all pressing to welcome their gracious and beautiful visitor. Her presence was still a novelty there at the time of Clarinda's first visits, for Mrs. Dillon had been but a few months a resident of that city; and Clari could not help noticing that, as time went on, the welcome grew less eager, the cheek did not flush, nor the eyes brighten with almost painful pleasure, on Mrs. Dillon's entrance, as they had been wont; the truthful heart of childhood refused to feign an attachment or a trust it could no longer feel.

The cause was soon apparent too.

"I must come next Saturday, and take you with me, my dear," Mrs. Dillon said one day, in Clari's hearing, to a poor little, fading, consumptive creature, whose hacking cough and hectic cheek told that another birthday would never be added to her eight short years.

The child's eyes beamed with rapture. "Would you like it so much?" Mrs. Dillon replied to their glance. "Then I will be sure to come. We will go to the park, and see the flowers and birds, and stay all day."

The week passed by. Clarinda happened to visit the asylum that Saturday, on a private errand of her own; she had undertaken a little special work of goodness, but was shy of its being known; indeed, that was the only fault I could ever lay to her charge—a too sensitive shrinking from observation; if she could only find some quiet corner where she might pursue her task unnoticed, she was quite happy. She had noticed that one of the children who joined in the singing had a voice unusually rich and clear, and she had asked the matron's leave to come once a week and lend what assistance she could to the cultivation of so rare a gift. Her offer was gladly accepted, and, the self-appointed task once begun, never did she falter in its fulfillment, more than recompensed by the warm and overflowing gratitude of her apt and docile pupil.

The lesson over, she was passing through the children's sitting-room, on her way out, when she caught sight of a little figure, half-buried in the cushions of a lounge, sobbing convulsively. She stepped hastily forward to learn the cause of such distress, when the child raised her head, and Clarinda recognized with astonishment the little girl to whom Mrs. Dillon had promised that bewitching holiday; the day had proved so charming that she had felt quite sure they were both enjoying the promised pleasure, especially as she knew Mrs. Dillon was in good health and spirits, and disengaged.

"Why, my poor little darling, what is the matter? You will make yourself quite ill by crying like this," Clarinda said, soothingly, drawing the trembling little frame within her gentle arms, and putting back the hair from the burning forehead.

"Oh, why—why did she not come?" sobbed the child, in a paroxysm of grief; "and I watched—I watched—for her—all day."

Clarinda's heart ached with indignation. "Poor little lamb! It was too hard, too hard," she said, hoping to soothe that hysterical passion of tears. A fearful fit of coughing seized the child as she spoke; she gasped, and panted, and grew so faint that Clarinda, in alarm, called the matron.

"I never saw a child take anything so much to heart," the good woman said, as she administered some quieting restorative. "I have been at my wit's end about her all day; I thought, by leaving her alone a while, and not seeming to notice, it would pass off; but she's just as bad as ever, and one can't use much authority with her, poor thing, she's so weakly like. There, there, my pretty, don't cry so; here's Miss Ross come to see you, if t'other lady hasn't. May be she'll tell you a story. I wish to goodness," she added under her breath, "such a fine visitor wouldn't make promises she doesn't mean to keep."

Clarinda laid aside her shawl and bonnet. She knew the matron was unusually busy that afternoon; her own day's work was over.

"I will stay for an hour, anyway," she said; "may be I can amuse her."

She knelt down beside the child, and after a little while succeeded in gaining her attention.

"I know such a pretty story," she said; "I wonder, would any little girl like to hear it?"

The child looked at her with speaking eyes, though the lips still quivered.

"But I can't tell it unless she will sit on my lap," Clarinda went on. "I wonder, wouldn't she like to hear all about that lovely glass slipper; but then I am tired and can't talk loud, and may be she won't sit on my lap—but I wish she would."

The little thin arms reached out to meet her own; the weak, unsteady voice said, plaintively, "I'll sit on your lap, Miss Ross," and her point was gained.

So, for more than an hour of that bright June evening she sat holding that wasted little form in a tender embrace, and rocking softly to and fro, while she told the dear old stories of Cinderella and the Sleeping Beauty, and sang sweet, pensive strains that lulled the child to sleep.

As she walked slowly home through the calm summer twilight, her thoughts unsullied by any self-approving gratulation, thankful only that she had been able to bestow some pleasure even on a child, I think her pain was almost as severe as if she herself had borne the pang of disappointment. Nay, was she not bearing the pang of a far deeper disappointment—the bitter pain that follows the first knowledge of defect in one we love.

"Yet, I may judge her wrongly," she thought humbly; "she may have had good reason."

A few days after she met Mrs. Dillon on the street; some casual observation recalled the little sufferer to the lady's mind.

"I declare," she said, "I entirely forgot I had promised to take that little Agnes to the park last Saturday. Some friends had called before lunch that day, and asked me to go and see their new house, and I couldn't refuse—they were so very pressing; and I never remembered till we were in the carriage. I am really sorry; but then another day will do her just as well. I hope she did not mind it much; I dare say a few sugar-plums will make it all right."

Clarinda said nothing. How could she? But her grave, clear eyes conveyed an unconscious reproach, from which Mrs. Dillon turned uneasily away, with a vague sense of shame and remorse.

Alas, this incident was but the type of many. Yet, to the casual observer, to those who only notice the world's outside life, Mrs. Dillon appeared as gracious, as generous in her benefactions, as the fairest "Lady Bountiful" that ever figured in the pages of history or romance. If an acquaintance met by chance her elegant chariot some soft spring day, and, pausing to return her beaming salutation, noticed the pale and interesting invalid, to whom she was giving an airing, reposing on those luxurious cushions by her side; did she not speak with enthusiasm of her sweet and unobtrusive charity, and liken her to beings of a purer sphere? If another, perhaps a mother, met her at the panorama, surounded by a rosy group of children, delighting in their delight, did she not utter soft praises of the lovely lady whose childless home failed to satisfy the tender yearnings of her nature? Yes, believe me, if we are prone to think evil, we are also prone to exaggerate good; and there is something in nearly every heart which responds with an overflow of pleasure to the tale of good deeds done, and is ready to argue from the glimpse revealed that untold self-denials, untold generosities, have been practiced unseen by vulgar eyes. So fared it with Mrs. Dillon. The kind acts which she certainly did perform with ready zeal, when nothing intervened to distract her attention, won for her an enviable name; and if the matron of the orphan asylum smothered her passing indignation; if the widow who fretted over the non-arrival of the warm suit of winter clothing that was so readily promised to the fatherless boy, and so singularly tardy in bestowal, hushed the repining that rose to her lips; if many who suffered the pain of a trivial or serious disappointment, refrained from any outward complaint, who shall blame their chosen silence, or unjustly speak of them as time-servers and cravens? Many and substantial, no doubt, were the favors they each and all received from that fair hand. It is not her lack of compassion or help of which I complain; it is of that heedless disregard for her own promises, that slight respect for her own word, which robbed all her good deeds of their most precious fruit, and sullied her own nature with the degradation of at least a seeming falsehood. For so it came to pass that, even among those she benefited most, her kindest messages and warmest assurances of help received but little credence until actually fulfilled; and how often, even among those sincerely grateful, was the disappointment more clearly remembered than the benefit.

Meanwhile the months followed each other swiftly on the track of time, and the first days of a beautiful summer found both Mrs. Dillon and Clarinda Ross inmates of the village where my sketch begins. Clarinda and her aunt had moved hither in obedience to the call and urgent entreaty of an old and faithful friend—a Mr. L.—who had been Clarinda's music master in her childhood and early girlhood. Even in that long ago time, she recalled him as bent and worn by years of toil, his mild face beaming on her under the crown of iron-grey hair. They had lost sight of one another since Clari herself had been borne away by the resistless tide of circumstances, to struggle with what bravery she might amid the surging multitude; but many and tender were the links of recollection still uniting them. Now, when health and strength were failing more surely every year, Mr. L. wrote, calling her back to the old home-work.

"It would grieve me much, my dear," he said, "to see my work pass into other hands than yours; so come, while I can still delegate it, and complete what I must leave unfinished. Here is honest work and honest compensation, and pleasant neighbors, and green fields, and fresh, restoring country air, waiting you—do not disappoint their welcome. And, if your aunt and you, my dearest Clari, my beloved pupil and old friend, can tolerate the whims and garrulous tempers of an old and lonely man, here is a quiet cottage that will brighten afresh in the sunshine of your presence."

That was a happy summer to Clarinda. The rose stole back to her cheek, which had paled in the close, confining city rooms; her eyes shone clear and bright as any child's. Her old master listened, with a smile upon his face, to the universal verdict acknowledging her ability as his successor; and the melody of her sweet young voice fell upon his ear as she led the singing in the grey old church, and awakened vague, tender thoughts of other harmonies heaven might grant him to listen to ere long. Ah, leal and loving soul! for thee the future holds no terror, no remorse. In the quiet paths thou trod on earth, thy gentle influence has blessed how many! Thy duties, never unfulfilled, have rebuked what faithless spirits!

Ah, here were no broken promises, no trust forfeited. The quiet current of this life had saved from sterile waste many a hidden nook, and even when it passed from earthly sight there were those who had daily cause to bless its thoughtful and tender beneficence. For when, that autumn, death softly closed the fading, weary eyes of the old music master, and released that childlike spirit from the trammels of an infirm mortality, to the perennial youth for which it yearned, Clarinda found herself the heir of that quaint little cottage and garden where she had met so warm a welcome months before, and of all the small wealth of which her old friend died possessed. It seemed real wealth to her, for it lifted herself and the aunt so dearly loved at once and forever above the dreary struggle "to make both ends meet," and, while the necessity for work was not removed, the terror of lacking it was no longer present; and a home—no lodging—but a real, real home 'round which her heart entwined its tendrils more closely every year; a treasure passionately yearned for, but beyond her hopes, was realized at last.

It may have been the contrast between Mrs. Dillon's life and that of the one whose last, lingering moments she had so lately shared, that touched Clarinda with so keen a sense of indignation and sorrow when her fair friend, following her usual impulsive fashion, made little Blossom her protege, pro tem. These summer months, during which Mrs. Dillon had fled to the country to recuperate for the winter's dissipation, were dull, no doubt, and she was glad of any object, of however slight an interest, which varied the monotony; while her passion for playing the generous and queenly benefactress, and winning that half-adoring gratitude which young hearts so readily bestow, might find full scope in that secluded spot.

* * * *

"What a lovely day you will have, Blossom!" said Isabel Maurice, awakening her little sister on the morning of the promised drive.

The child turned on her feverish pillow, and opened her large, bright eyes, beaming with delight; they lit up the wan little face with too intense a glory, Bella thought, pained, she scarce knew why; and she sighed as she noticed how thin, how very thin, the small arms were that answered her caress.

"Mamma," she said that day, "do you think Blossom is any worse than usual? Somehow, I fancied this morning that she looked more fevered and spent than before."

Mrs. Maurice's eyes filled with tears, and Bella saw that she was much disquieted, and questioned her no more; that strange silence falling between them which tells that each is conscious of, but unable to shape into words, the other's dread.

Still, when the child was brought down stairs, all flushed with the excitement of the promised joy, mother and sisters forgot their anxiety in her delight and amusing impatience.

"Oughtn't you to dress me right away, Jenny?" she said; "for, you know, may be Mrs. Dillon will come very, very soon."

"Why, you little goose," laughed the indulgent elder sister, "you don't suppose Mrs. Dillon is as eager for a drive as you are? But come, we won't risk any delay."

Alas, poor little Blossom! Nine o'clock came—ten—eleven—still no ring at the door, no sound of wheels upon the road. Bella came home from her weekly practicing with Clari and others at the old church. She found the trembling, expectant child lying on her sofa by the window, straining wistful eyes to catch a glimpse of the wished-for carriage.

"Don't fret, dear," Bella said, cheeringly. "Mrs Dillon may have been busy; she will be sure to come this afternoon. There is mamma calling us to dinner—let me help you. You know Mrs. Dillon can't come now for an hour, so try and eat a little; and then I will brush your hair out nice and smooth—oh, what a tangled Blossom you are!—and you will be all fresh and bright when the carriage comes."

"Oh, Bella," Blossom whispered eagerly, "do you think she will come—do you, really? No one ever promised me a drive before, and you can't think how I long for it."

"Of course she will come, you foolish little Blossom!" Bella answered confidently, but her heart ached as she thought how true the child's words were. All their friends were in moderate circumstances, like themselves, and much as many of them might wish to bestow such a kindness, much as Mrs. Maurice's own heart yearned over her afflicted child, neither she nor they dared afford the luxury of such indulgence. So Blossom's visits to the outside world were confined to a journey round the garden, where, in fine weather, Bella would wheel her gently—for any rough motion jarred her sensitive frame—in a garden chair, over the smooth walks.

Well, the day passed on, and hour by hour hope faded out from the patient little heart. The long, delicious summer twilight darkened to its close, and through the evening quiet came the roll of wheels and merry voices in laughter and talk; and Mrs. Dillon's carriage swept past, filled with a gay and elegant party of ladies and gentlemen, loaded with fragrant treasures from the flower show.

Blossom's cheek flushed and paled as she watched them pass, and the soft summer air carried wafts of faint perfume through the open window. "Oh, dear," she sighed, not petulantly, not complainingly, but with such a pathos of disappointed trust; and one large tear fell slowly down her cheek.

* * * *

There were hurried footsteps that night in Mrs. Maurice's chamber, and anxious faces watching the delirious slumbers of the childish sufferer. I know not whether the crisis of those long years of pain and trial had arrived before, or whether that bitter pang of hope deferred had hurried on the final hour. Poor Mrs. Maurice always believed the latter to be the truth. Be it as it may, no skill availed to save the faded flower—no cherishing love might bid the blighted Blossom unfold her closing leaves.

Two days later, Mrs. Dillon, meeting Clarinda, learned the story of the child's illness.

"Poor little thing!" she exclaimed, really shocked and pained by the sudden tidings. "Is there no hope, Clari, of her recovery? I am so grieved—more than I can say—to have failed in giving her that one holiday; but really, I did not see how to help it. My cousin had only arrived the evening before, and a large party of friends were asking my company for that one day—they must leave the next morning. I fully intended taking Blossom out some day this week, to make amends."

"I am very sorry," said Clarinda simply, and could not help adding a little coldly, "If you could have sent your maid to tell Mrs. Maurice your change of plan, it might have saved poor Blossom much needless pain."

"But I never thought," plead Mrs. Dillon. "I was so hurried; and a child's passing disappointment seems a thing so easily rectified."

"Yet it is a more serious pain than you imagine," Clarinda said, constrained to speak more plainly than her wont, "especially to a sensitive nature. You, to whom a ride is a pleasure of daily occurrence, can form no idea of the charm with which an imaginative, delicate child invests the fulfillment of such a promise."

"You speak so gravely," answered Mrs. Dillon. "You—you judge me harshly, Clarinda."

Her lips actually quivered, half with wounded pride and feeling, half with slowly awakening remorse.

"If I felt as you do, I should never dare to promise anything, for fear of possible failure in keeping my word."

"I did not mean to hurt you," Clari said gently; "but, indeed, I only spoke what I know to be truth, and very often, believe me, less evil is wrought by promises unmade than by promises made and broken."

She was too wise and too kind to linger longer to dispute the point, and, with a hurried "good morning," hastened away.

Mrs. Dillon gazed after her, her eyes full of vexed and angry tears, astonished to find herself at all reproved by another. Indeed, Clarinda, however her quiet manner might reveal disapprobation, had always delicately refrained from interfering in any way with Mrs. Dillon's bestowal, or non-bestowal, of kindness, no matter how obviously the passing of opinion might be thrust upon her. But here, her aunt's old friendship for Mrs. Maurice, her own fond affection for all the family, seemed to justify her in speaking more plainly her thought. Yet she did it, not in any heat of resentment — perhaps with indignation, but with bitter pain and reluctance, too.

"I have lost her friendship forever," she

murmured, as she turned away, "forever! and I loved her dearly, too! But how could I say less?"

That afternoon, Mrs. Dillon's servant left at Mrs. Maurice's door the loveliest bouquet that tasteful hands had ever gathered, and a basket of the rarest white grapes from the clustering vines of the hothouse.

"With Mrs. Dillon's compliments; and she begged to know if the little girl was better."

She had not been able, from very shame, to come herself to make the inquiry. She was astonished at the tumult of thought and feeling which that talk with Clari had awakened; and tried vainly to dull the edge of her regrets by offerings like these.

"No better, thank you," Jenny answered the maid, with quiet sadness; and sent their acknowledgments for Mrs. Dillon's kindness.

"I wonder you took the things!" poor, impulsive, broken-hearted Bella said, angrily, as Jenny closed the door. "We do not want her presents now. I hate her gracious ways—I hate her!" She broke down in smothered sobbings.

"Bella—Bella! don't dear!" Jenny whispered. "She has done wrong, I own, not to send us word; but may be she has excuse for her neglect, and is sorry now—oh, she may well be sorry! And poor little Blossom—I thought the fruit and flowers might amuse her, and do some good."

She carried them softly into the sickroom. The delirium was over now; the large eyes looked out clearly and intelligently from the pallid, pallid face; the small, thin hands lay nerveless on the coverlet; her smile still answered theirs again; her faint voice spoke to them; her trembling lips repeated their caress, and yet, they knew there was no hope—no hope! Oh, hope for thee, sweet Blossom! that soon thou shalt have passed to the tender arms of Him who suffers little children, and forbids them not, the heaven of His presence, where pain and weariness are known no more forever.

"See what Mrs. Dillon has sent you, darling!" Jenny said softly, bending over the bed. "Try and taste some of these nice cool grapes; and look, what beautiful flowers! She is so sorry she could not come for you, that day; but may be, when you are well again—"

"When I am well again," the child repeated, toying absently with the gifts—"when I am well again!" And she fixed her wistful gaze upon her sister's face. Jenny could not bear that mute interrogation, and turned her head aside.

That night the struggle ended, and the peace of death fell upon the fragile frame so long tortured by the anguish of disease. The morning light revealed to Mrs. Dillon, standing at her chamber window, the long streamer of white crape fluttering from the window far down across the street. She felt a sudden heart convulsion as she looked; and some old words she had long forgotten came into her mind unbidden: "Let your yea be yea, and your nay nay, for whatsoever is more than these cometh of evil." And something whispered to her awakened consciousness, "Aye, and whatsoever is less than these—comes it not of evil, too? For what thy hand findeth to do, that do—not carelessly, not indifferently—but with thy might; for the night draws on."

A few hours later, she stood where Mrs. Maurice watched beside her child. She stammered some words of wonted sympathy, some phrases of condolence; then raising the lid of the basket on her arm, revealed—what treasures of snowy roses, of pure lilies of the valley, heart's-ease, violets, all that might image forth the innocent young life whose earthly bloom was ended.

"Please allow me," she began, with deft hand beginning to remove her tribute from its basket. But Mrs. Maurice, with a sudden, imperative, gentle movement, arrested her.

"Pardon me," she said, "but I could not bear it."

She thought of that crystal tear on the cheek of her poor, patient darling; and turned away, with loathing almost, from all that largesse of fragrant loveliness brought to deck her bier.

These last few days had revealed many strange phases of thought and feeling to Mrs. Dillon. The grief of a child had seemed a trifling matter—to be considered, if nothing more important hindered. It had suddenly assumed a dignity, an anguish of its own—as real as those of graver troubles. And now she saw that older hearts might be struck through and through with cruel pain by that same childish grief which she had slighted so often—ah, how often! The mother's sorrow, the gentleness of her implied reproach, touched and awed her; her whole life rose up suddenly before her, in all its false disguise of counterfeit tenderness and charity for others; the retrospect shocked and startled her. With a sudden impulse, she kissed Mrs. Maurice's hand; a tear fell on it—a mute petition for pardon, a mute witness of her new resolve. Then she was gone.

"God help me!" she said humbly, as she went out—"God help me!"

Was it the first time she had invoked such help, in all the days so full of self-applause, in all her endeavor to gain the praise of others?

I know not if her life redeemed its broken promise, through coming years; we leave her with those words, so fit for faltering mortal tongue, upon her lips and in her heart—and are they not a prophecy and a pledge for all her future?

www.ingramcontent.com/pod-product-compliance
Lightning Source LLC
Chambersburg PA
CBHW020125170426
43199CB00009B/634